THE REPUBLICAN-DEMOCRAT POLITICAL CAMPAIGNS

IN TEXAS IN 1964

by

JACK CRICHTON

First published by AuthorHouse 05/21/04

ISBN:1-4184-5586-5 (e-book)
ISBN: 1-4184-2574-5 (Paperback)

This book is printed on acid free paper.

TABLE OF CONTENTS

FOREWORD

I, Jack Crichton, was flattered when I was asked by an archivist at Baylor University, Waco, Texas, to give them my files from my campaign for Governor of Texas in 1964.

Baylor, with its excellent law school, has produced a number of governors of Texas over the years, and for my files to be included in that prestigious history was exciting. However, when the George Bush Presidential Library was awarded to my Alma Mater, Texas A&M University, College Station, Texas, and since George Bush had been a fellow Republican candidate in 1964, I contacted the Director of Texas A&M Library, Mrs. Irene Hoadley, and offered the files to Texas A&M. She accepted, and was making arrangements to secure them; then I decided that an explanation of some of the events that occurred in that campaign was necessary to make them worthwhile.

Accordingly, I asked her to delay their procurement until I had finished using them as a reference.

It seemed to me that some of the events that occurred were important historical happenings in which I had some knowledge. Such events were the visit of President Kennedy to Dallas in November 1963, and his subsequent assassination; my visit to ex-Governor Coke Stevenson at his ranch outside of Junction, Texas, and his story of the infamous Box 13, Wells County,

Texas, votes that sent Lyndon Johnson to the U.S. Senate (a necessary step in his becoming president) the association with George Bush; the media campaign that destroyed the presidential aspirations of Senator Barry Goldwater, and the establishment of a base by the Republican Party to make Texas a two party state. Therefore, I decided to write my recollection of these events.

CHAPTER 1

BECOMING A CANDIDATE

It was the summer of 1963 in Dallas, and I was busy at that time as President of a private independent oil and gas company, and of a petroleum consulting company. My career up to that time had included attending and graduating from Texas A&M in 1937 with a Bachelor of Science Degree in Petroleum Engineering, and with a commission as a Second Lieutenant in the United States Army Reserve; attending and graduating from the Massachusetts Institute of Technology in 1938 with a Masters Degree in Petroleum Engineering; working during the summers as a laborer in the oil fields of Texas; working as a geologist-engineer in Texas and Louisiana form 1938-1941; serving five years in the U.S. Army, Army Air Corps, Army Intelligence, and office of Strategic Services (the forerunner of the Central Intelligence Agency,) and being discharged in 1946 as a Major, U.S. Army Intelligence after service in five battle campaigns in Europe. After the military service working for the prestigious consulting firm of DeGolyer & Mac Naughton, Dallas, Texas, first as a geologist engineer, then as Vice President and Director until 1950 when I helped form and build up an oil and gas producing firm named San Juan Oil Company, which was sold to General American Oil company two years later at a substantial profit; then heading up a public company called Oil & Gas Property Management,

1

which bought more than $100 million of petroleum properties from 1952 to 1959. The company was sold at a price returning ten for one in equity to its shareholders, and finally establishing my own petroleum consulting firm and oil and gas company.

In addition, I had married an attractive former Braniff stewardess, had two small daughters, ages ten and eight, had kept up my Army activities and was now a Colonel, U.S. Army Intelligence Reserve. I had also been active in local Republican politics, as had my wife, Marilyn, and in alumni affairs at Texas A&M, and in 1963 was Vice President of the Association of Former Students. I was also concerned about the left wing tilting of the foreign policy of the United States under the Democratic Administration, having personally visited Cuba during Batista days just before Castro's takeover, and having made speeches in Dallas about Castro's Communists affiliation when he was being hailed as the George Washington of Cuba. I list all these things because they were important factors in my becoming the Republican candidate for Governor of Texas.

In August 1963, I received a telephone call from my close friend, Ed Monteith, an A&M alumnus friend, and head of the Oil and Gas Department of the Republic Bank, Dallas. (Ed and I and Jimmy Aston, President of Republic Bank and also an A&M alumnus, had formed a corporation called AMC Corporation, an oil financing company, in which all of the profits went to the Texas A&M to support such things as bonuses to outstanding professors, which ultimately awarded some $250,000 to A&M.) Ed asked me to meet him that afternoon for coffee at Vick's Restaurant on the ground floor of the Vaughn Building. I met Ed, and with him were Josephine Kanowsky, a member of the State Republican Executive Committee, and Pat Holloway, a young Yale graduate lawyer with Thompson & Knight, a leading law firm in Dallas.

Ed introduced Josephine Kanowsky, and she immediately made her pitch: "Texas is going to be a key state in the election of the next President. We believe that whoever is the Republican candidate for Governor of Texas will have a great deal of influence on the number of votes our Presidential candidate will have, which we expect to be Barry Goldwater. We've done some research on you, and believe you can be a factor in getting Texas for Goldwater. We know you are slated to be President of the Association of Former Students of Texas A&M next year; you've been President of the Association of the U.S. Army in Texas and can swing some military votes. You've been an officer in the Independent Petroleum Association and can attract some blue collar votes, and though you've never held a political office, we think that this will attract votes with some people who would rather see an engineer executive be Governor then the usual lawyer."

Pat Holloway chimed in, "As a lawyer, I would second that last statement. "I'll help with the money raising," Ed said.

I then said, "I'm flattered that you would even consider me as a candidate, but John Connally, the current Governor, has a lock on the political money, is known as a conservative Democrat, is a handsome University of Texas alum, attracts a lot of the ladies votes, and has not made any grievous mistakes as Governor."

Josephine interrupted to say, "He has come vulnerabilities. He has had politically to go along with some of the national Democratic policies, which are an anathema to many Texans. And thus, Connally's close ties with LBJ make him vulnerable."

Josephine then said, "Well, think about it and let me know something."

I replied, "Well thank you Josephine for even considering me. I'm in shock right now. Let's have some more coffee."

The following week I reviewed my business. Dallas Resources was a producing oil and gas company with settled oil and gas production from a number of wells in Texas, Oklahoma and Louisiana. Crichton & Company was an oil and gas consulting and management company that my associates could operate with my checking in weekly on problems that might develop.

I then turned my attention to the national political scene. As a colonel in the Army Intelligence Reserves, I had been concerned about the takeover in Cuba by Castro. I had been in Cuba on an oil concession management contract during the Batista era, and knew that one of the reasons for its failure was President's Kennedy's decision to call off the air strike that enabled Castro's tanks to decimate the Cuban Landing Forces. This greatly troubled me as to President Kennedy's ability to defend the United States against the Soviet empire. Thus, I thought that if I could be of help to the campaign of Senator Goldwater to become President it would be worthwhile.

I analyzed the political situation in Texas. In the previous gubernatorial election in 1962, John Connally, a Democrat, defeated Jack Cox, a Republican by a vote of 847,000 to 715,000 in a very close race. Cox was a former conservative Democrat who could not go along with the leftist policies of the National Democrat Party.

Cox had opted to run for the Senate in 1944 and would face George H.W. Bush in the Republican primary.

I talked to my neighbor, Hughes Brown, who had served in the Texas House of Representatives about running for Governor.

Hughes said, "You will be an underdog with no name recognition but I think you'd make a good candidate if you decide to do it, I'll be happy to pitch in and help."

I later talked to my business associates, and they all assured me they could run the business if I decided to run.

In early September I decided to be a candidate for Governor of the great State of Texas.

I telephoned Josephine Kanowsky to let the Republican State Executor Committee know that I would be a candidate. She seemed pleased and pledged her help to me.

In September and October I got my affairs in order so that I would devote most of my time to preparing myself for the campaign.

CHAPTER 2

THE ASSASSINATION OF PRESIDENT AND THE WOUNDING OF GOVERNOR JOHN CONNALLY

In the presidential election of 1960, the key states that led to Kennedy's election were Illinois and Texas. Texas was brought to Kennedy's total by Lyndon Johnson, the Vice Presidential candidate, and his well organized political organization in Texas.

But in the coming election, Johnson had lost much of his political prowess in Texas. As a result, the Kennedy political planners thought it was imperative to bolster Kennedy's popularity in Texas by a visit to Texas. Therefore, a swing through Texas was organized.

After stops in Houston and San Antonio, the entourage stopped on November 21st in Fort Worth. After a warm reception there, they proceeded by Air Force One to Dallas Love Field.

At that time, I was President of the Dallas A&M Club. For years, it had been the tradition of the Dallas A&M club and the University Longhorn Club to alternate in hosting of each at a luncheon on the Friday preceding the next Thursday's Thanksgiving football game. At each luncheon there was satire demeaning the other school's team.

Thus, on November 22nd at about 11:00, I left my office in the Vaughn building on Commerce Street and walked toward the Adolphus Hotel where the luncheon was to be held. Enroute, I walked over to Elm Street to see the Kennedy delegation as it proceeded to the luncheon for the President in the Trade Mart.

As the motorcade came down Elm Street, President Kennedy and Jackie made a handsome couple. She was resplendent in her pink dress and pink pillbox hat. The crowds on the sidewalks applauded, and waved as they drove by. After they passed where I was standing, I continued to walk to the Adolphus Hotel on Commerce Street.

I entered the hotel and went to the French Room; site of the A&M-Texas luncheon. The room was almost filled, and people were seated at the individual tables. I proceeded to the head table, and greeted the fellow officers of the A&M Club.

Afterwards, I went to the wings to see if our performer had arrived. Our performer was a dancer we had hired to appear at the proper time.

That year the different schools had stolen mascots including the Rice Owl, and Peruna the pony horse from SMU. Our skit was that we had stolen the Harvard mascot. (A pretty girl who had accompanied Kennedy to Dallas.) She was dressed in clinging fabric, and said she was ready to come on stage whenever called.

We had the invocation, and many guests began to eat their lunch.

Suddenly we heard sirens screaming and someone from outside ran up to the head table and excitedly said, "The President, Vice President, and Governor Connally have all been shot."

I stood and announced this news. There was stunned silence in the room. Someone then produced a radio, and heard the news confirmed that the President had been shot.

Those people in the audience who dealt in stocks and bonds rushed to get to their offices since they knew there would be much selling. The remainder of the crowd sat in stunned silence listening to the continuing news on the radio.

I went backstage and paid the dancer fifty dollars, and told her she could go. (Years later I was at a cocktail party in New York and was introduced to a couple as someone from Dallas, Texas. The lady said "I was a dancer in Dallas at that time and was supposed to do a skit when the President was shot. The man in charge paid me fifty dollars and said you can go now." I said, "Believe it or not, I was the guy that paid you the fifty dollars.")

The crowd slowly returned to their work place. I walked from the Adolphus Hotel back to my office in the Vaughn Building.

There was chaos in the streets. Drivers speeding to get to their homes, groups gathered around a blaring radio. I proceeded to my office, and when I got there immediately called my wife, Marilyn, to tell her I would be coming home soon.

When I arrived at my house on Kenshire Lane, North Dallas, my daughter, Anne, age 10, and Cathy, age 8 had come home from school. The family watched television in awed silence.

At approximately six o'clock I received a call from Colonel George Lumpkin, Deputy Chief of Police of Dallas. George and I had been friends for years. He was active in Army Reserve Officers, and knew that I commanded an Army Reserve Intelligence Unit.

He said, "Do you have any members of your unit that speak Russian fluently enough to come down here and act as the interpreter in questioning Marina Oswald?"

I said, "I have some good Russian translators but no one expert enough to do what you need."

George said, "I need someone right away. Any suggestions?"

"Yes, I have a Russian friend, Ilya Mamintov, who is a geologist with Sun Oil Company. He has some family still in Russia, but he might be reticent to get involved."

"Call him immediately," George said.

This I did. Ilya answered the phone, and said he would be pleased to be of assistance. He also stated he knew the Oswald's and could tell the police something about them.

I relayed this information to George, who then sent a squad car out to pick up Ilya. (Later it was disclosed that Ilya's wife was returning from the grocery store and saw her husband being whisked away in a Dallas police car with sirens screaming. She later said she almost had a heart attack when she saw this happening.)

Ilya acted as the interpreter in the questioning of Marina Oswald on Friday and Saturday.

On Sunday after Jack Ruby shot Oswald, Ilya telephoned me at my house on Kenshire Lane and said he would like to come to my house and discuss his experience.

This he did, and he was visibly shaken by the experience.

Apparently Captain Will Fritz asked the question of Marina, and Ilya acted as the interpreter when needed.

"How did you know the Oswald's," I asked.

Ilya said, "There's a small Russian community in Dallas, and there's a social gathering almost every week. The Oswald's were frequently there. My mother-in-law was also teaching Russian to Mrs. Ruth Paine, with whom the Oswald's were staying. I was always suspect of Oswald because when he was between jobs, he always seemed to have an income from somewhere, and I thought he probably was an intelligence agent of some kind."

"How did Marina respond?"

"She was obviously shaken, but answered the important questions quite forcefully."

Ilya then said, "The police would bring Oswald out at times to show the media he was not being mistreated and I feared that if there was a conspiracy in which Oswald was a part, he would be eliminated." Thus, I was not surprised when Jack Ruby shot Oswald this morning."

Shortly afterwards, Ilya left and Marilyn and the girls returned to watch the news on television. (I remember that Eddie Barker seemed to be the most credible on television.)

Dallas was a city in a state of shock. The eastern newspapers and media blamed the assassination on the "right wing element" in Dallas.

The nation paused to observe the television broadcast of the funeral services.

The next week, I went to New York on a business trip. After arriving at LaGuardia airport, I took a cab to go to my hotel downtown.

We had traveled one block when in making conversation, this cabbie said, "Where are you from?"

"Dallas", I said.

He stopped the cab, pulled over to the curb and said, "Get Out."

This was the mood of the country.

The Eastern media blamed the assassination on the "right wing" in Dallas. The televised funeral memorializing President Kennedy gripped the nation. The rider less horse, little John Kennedy saluting at his father's casket, and the stoic demeanor of Jacqueline were mind boggling.

Citizens called for immediate vengeance, and selected Dallas as the target. The Soviet Union, the Mafia, and the Cubans betrayed at the Bay of Pigs came in second.

The reasons for blaming Dallas could be traced to several causes. One was an incident in which United Nations Ambassador and former Presidential candidate Adlai Stevenson was reported "spit on" and hit with a sign in October 1963 in Dallas. Another was an incident in which Bruce Alger, Republican Congressman from Dallas, led a demonstration against Lyndon Johnson who was entering the Adolphus Hotel in which reportedly Lyndon Johnson and his wife Lady Bird, were jostled by the crowd.

Dallas had been a stronghold for Vice President Richard Nixon and Nixon was reportedly having lunch at the home of oilman Clint Murchison in Dallas the day before President Kennedy was shot.

Dallas had also been the center for right wing publications such as Life Line, published by oilman H.L. Hunt.

A full page newspaper ad had appeared in the Dallas Morning News on the occasion of President Kennedy's visit to Dallas that "attacked" the CIA for arranging a coup against Deim in Vietnam and having anti-communist allies of the U.S. exterminated.

The episode of Jack Ruby shooting Oswald on television in the Dallas Police basement had led the rest of the United States to believe that Dallas was indeed a rogue city where no one was safe.

Lyndon Johnson was sworn in as President by Judge Hughes on the afternoon of November 22nd in the Air Force One, and immediately acted as President of the United States.

By executive order #11130, dated November 30, 1993, President Johnson appointed a commission to report upon the assassination of President John F. Kennedy.

The Commission consisted of a Chairman, the Chief Justice of the United States, Earl Warren, Senator Richard B. Russell (Georgia), Senator John Thomas Cooper (Kentucky), Congressman Hale Boggs (Louisiana) Congressman Gerald B. Ford (Michigan), The Honorable Allen W. Dulles (CIA) the Honorable John McCloy (Ex-Assistant Secretary of War.)

The general counsel was J. Lee Rankin, former Solicitor general of the United States.

The Commission moved quickly to investigate. The FBI submitted it's initial report on December 9, 1963.

Since there were rumors that the Soviet Union or Castro Cubans staged the assassination, President Johnson wanted an early report to show that they were not the guilty parties, but the work of a lone gunman. Otherwise, the public would require action against the Soviet Union or Cuba.

As the Commanding Officers of an active Army Reserve Strategic Intelligence Unit, and as the intelligence officer for the Dallas County Civil Defense team, of which Colonel John Mayo was chairman, the results of the investigation were important to me.

Was the assassination the first step by the Russians in a war against the United States?

The Aerial information that resulted in the removal of nuclear weapons from Cuba to the chagrin of Chairman Kruschev was much in the memory of the citizens of Dallas.

At the instigation of Civil Defense, downtown office buildings had in their basement stores of water and emergency rations, and a number of bomb shelters were built in back yards.

The investigation was carried on by the FBI. When the assassination was committed, it was not a federal offense but a crime under the jurisdiction of local authorities. The Dallas Police Department acted according to this authority after the event, but subsequently they were almost excluded by the FBI, and it became apparent to interested observers that evidence that did not support the lone gunman theory was not being considered.

The Commission did not issue its final report until September 25, 1964, and concluded that the assassination was the work of one man, Lee Harvey Oswald, and there was no conspiracy, foreign or domestic.

In the meantime, I followed the various the reports closely. I stayed in touch with my friend George Lumpkin, friends in army intelligence, and with a number of sources. One such source was Paul Rothemel, a lawyer and ex-FBI agent who was H.L. Hunts security advisor. Mr. Hunt, an oilman and internationally known was vitally interested in the Communist movement, and knowing I was in Army Intelligence, would contact me from time to time of my opinion of happenings in the Communist World.

Paul Rothemel told me that at one time, Jim Garrison, the New Orleans attorney who pursuing the case had Mr. Hunt as a suspect in financing the assassination. Paul said Garrison later withdrew his suspicion.

CHAPTER 3

ANNOUNCING MY BECOMING A CANDIDATE

On January 25, 1964, I was elected to be President of the 40,000 member Texas A&M Association of Former Students, and John Lindsey of Houston was elected as Vice President.

This was a great honor, and having served as Vice President, I had some ideas that I thought would expand the activities of the Association.

I then had to make a decision. The assassination of President Kennedy and the wounding of John Connally had changed the political spectrum in Texas. The odds on my being elected as Governor and Goldwater as President had changed completely. Should I go forward with the candidacy, or should I concentrate on doing a good job as President of the Association of Former Students.

I conferred with Hughes Brown, my campaign manager to be. Hughes said, "You will have an uphill battle, but you will have a chance to advance the cause of the Republican Party in Texas, and in politics anything can happen."

Thus, after talking to my wife Marilyn, I needed to resign as President of the Association and donate my energy to representing the Republican Party in a credible way in the race for Governor.

I telephoned Hughes and said, "OK Hughes, I've decided to go for it."

Hughes said, "We need to get started right away. The first step will be to go to Austin and pay $1000 to the Republican State Committee.

I then called Josephine Kanowsky and told her that I had not changed my mind since our first meeting about being a candidate for governor, but I was forced to consider not being a candidate after the Kennedy assassination and my election as President of the Association of Former Students at Texas A&M.

"I'm delighted", she said.

I then called the Executive Secretary of the Association, Buck Weirus to tell him of my decision.

"We're sorry you cannot serve but we understand", was the reply.

I then called John Lindsey in Houston, Vice President, to tell him that he would now become President.

I remember John saying, "I was looking forward to a year as Vice President so I would be prepared to be President.

Years later at an A&M meeting John told me that he would never forgive me for what I had done to him.

"Like what?" I asked.

"Well, at the first general meeting of the Association, President Rudder just before the meeting told me to offer a motion to allow women to attend the University. Since this was a much debated subject, with much opposition with some trepidation, I made the motions. I said, "All in favor" and there were a few yeses. Now *all opposed*" and there was a thunderous reply. I brought down the gavel down on the stand and announced the motion passes."

"That's how women were admitted to A&M and there are still some of my classmates who won't speak to me."

John went on to serve out his presidency with distinction, and later on was responsible for the founding of the A&M University Press, and was an important factor in getting the George Bush Presidential Library at A&M, and his lovely wife, Sarah, joined him in these endeavors.

On February 3rd, I went to Austin and paid my $1000 to the Republican State Treasurer. Hughes had called a press conference and there were a number of reporters there.

I was the second candidate to enter the race. Mr. C.G. Weakley, an insurance man, had already announced he would be a candidate, but I was the first to file.

When the reporters asked me what I would hope to accomplish if I became governor, I told them I was "dedicated to the principles of free enterprise and limited government and would offer a platform of a conservative economic and political philosophy."

CHAPTER 4

BEGINNING THE CAMPAIGN

On our return to Dallas, Hughes who was still a State Representative said, "We've go to put together a campaign staff."

With Hughes help, we assembled the following:

Dr. Dan Sutherland, Finance Manager, Paul Dearmin, Organizational Director, Taber Ward (Austin) News Releases, Publicity and Relationships in Austin, Warren Carroll, Speech Writer, Burgess Advertising Company; Advertising, Earl Foster, Archives.

Hughes arranged for office headquarters at 7007 Preston Road which comprised one half floor. We commenced with two full time secretaries. A TWX machine was installed there, as was one in a small office in Austin occupied by Tabor Ward.

"We now need to get you some name identification in the State", said Hughes. "This will involve getting handbills printed stating your stand on issues, calling on newspaper editors and Precinct Chairmen."

Duke Burgess put together an excellent small picture booklet that showed my educational, army and professional background as an engineer and executive, who was for better education in the State; opposition to a State income tax and other matters that were important to voters.

After this brochure was prepared, I called on Peter O'Donnell, the

Republican State Chairman.

Peter was a very "savvy" innovative person with strong convictions as to getting the right Republicans into political office.

His entrance in the political ring was by helping a friend, Bruce Alger of Dallas, in his race for Congress in 1954. Peter was a neophyte in the political arena, and it is reported that he obtained a copy of the CIO's political handbook on how to win elections and followed it story and verse. His effort got Bruce Alger elected.

Peter had been the Dallas County Chairman, and was now State Chairman, with strong ties to the election of Goldwater for President. Peter should be credited as the Father of the Republican Party in Texas.

After reviewing my brochure, he advised me to stress my experience as an engineer in helping design the largest gas storage facility in the United States, and that with my executive background could bring efficiency to the State Government.

After I had gotten some publicity stating my stand on key issues, I received a call from my opponent Clair Weakley, who said, "You have the same political agenda as I do, so rather than our spending our money in the primary, I've decided to withdraw my name and support you." This was welcome news. Clair then became my assistant campaign manager.

As a past President of the Dallas A&M Club and a past President of the Engineers Club in Dallas, and having given a number of petroleum engineering talks to large audiences, I was used to making speeches to large audiences.

Hughes said, "It is now time to get your feet wet. I've arranged a speaking engagement at College Station, the home of your Alma Mater and you should get a welcome reception there."

This it did, but afterwards I realized that political public speaking required a different approach. The audience wants to hear that you endorse the same issues in which they are interested, and "sound bites" are a necessary item.

After returning to Dallas, Hughes suggested I go to Austin and review the library of the Texas Research League. They have done extensive studies on the "pros and cons" of all issues that are of importance to the State Government of Texas. This I did, beginning with a study of the State Constitution. As a result of my visit, I formed my own platform as to the methods of State taxation, whether sales or property; the role of the state in education; the role of the state in regulating oil and gas production; the importance of the highway system; the benefits of no state income tax, the importance of tourism; the water problems in West Texas and a host of other subjects.

Now Hughes and I jointly selected a number of cities and towns in which to meet precinct chairman and make speeches that would get media coverage.

During the next few weeks I traveled almost 20,000 miles by plane and car visiting some 34 different cities and towns. For some of the larger cities several visits, the places included Richardson, Houston, Waco, Victoria, Dallas, Lubbock, Midland, Oak Cliff, Corpus Christi, Austin, Pampas, Perryton, Stratford, Dumas, Amarillo, Borger, El Paso, Galveston, College Station, Fort Worth, Brownsville, McAllen, Denton, Wolfe City, Marshall,

Longview, Tyler, Angleton, New Braunsfel, Bryan, Sherman, Brady, Odessa and Wichita Falls. In total I gave 65 speeches stressing the need for a two party system in Texas and a conservative approach to government.

In all these places I met people who were enthusiastic as to the brand of Republicanism I represented.

CHAPTER 5

THE PRIMARIES

The first primary was on May 2, 1964. I was unopposed.

There was a race to be the Republican candidate for the U.S. Senate.

There were four candidates for this office. Dr. Milton Davis, a prominent Dallas physician, Dr. Robert Morris, a conservative journalist, Jack Cox, a former Democrat who had been narrowly defeated by John Connally in the race for Governor in 1962, and George H.W. Bush who had moved to Midland after graduating from Yale, and who became the Republican County Chairman in Midland before moving to Houston where he was president of Zapata Offshore Company, a drilling contract company.

Jack Cox had the advantage of name identification and publicity from his race in 1962 when he was defeated by Connally in a fairly close race.

Bush was the son of a former U.S. Senator from Connecticut. He was very articulate and had a great deal of charisma. He also had the better campaign organization but had the disadvantage of being a transplanted Yankee.

Both candidates backed Senator Goldwater.

Concurrently with the Republican Primary, the State Executive committees had voted to have a presidential preferable ballot in conjunction with the May primary.

This was designed to helping the nominations for President of Barry Goldwater.

When the Houston Post endorsed George Bush for Senator in April 25th, it seemed to turn the tide in favor of Bush.

The results of the primary voting showed Bush with 62,000, Cox with 45,000, Robert Morris with 28,000, and Dr. Davis with 6,000. Thus, a runoff was necessary.

The preferential poll for president showed an overwhelming vote for Goldwater as against Ambassador Henry Cabot Lodge and Nelson Rockefeller.

On the runoff between Bush and Cox, on June 6, Bush got 49,000 votes and Cox 30,000. Thus, Bush became the Republican candidate for the Senate.

The Democratic primaries resulted in John Connally besting Don Yarbrough by 1,125,000 to 471,000 for Governor, and Ralph Yarborough besting Gordon McLendon for the U.S. Senate.

Thus in the general election it would be me versus Connally and Bush verses Yarbrough.

CHAPTER 6

THE REPUBLICAN CONVENTION

The Republican National Convention was held in San Francisco from July 13-17, 1964.

The State of Texas had 65 delegates who were pledged to support the nomination of Senator Goldwater unless released by the Chairman of the delegation-Senator Tower.

The convention was held at the Cow Palace. Most of the Texas delegates stayed at the Jack Tar Hotel or the Mark Hopkins.

Peter O'Donnell, State Chairman, had been instrumental in persuading Senator Goldwater to be a candidate and had a great deal of influence on the platform adopted.

The convention was a contest between the Eastern Liberal Republicans delegates supporting Governor Nelson Rockefeller, and the central, western and southern delegates supporting Senator Goldwater.

From Texas, National Committeeman Albert Fay and former national Committee Woman Barbara Mann were on the Credentials Committee. (The current national Committee Woman was Mrs. Flo Kampman.) Serving on the Rules and Order Business Committee were George Bush and State Vice Chairman Kathryn McDaniel. Beryl Milburn and I were on the Permanent Organization Committee, U.S. Senator John Tower and Anne Armstrong were on the most important committee - the Resolution Committee which would determine the party platform.

The first order of business was the Credentials Committee to determine the makeup of the convention. Then there was a debate on the platform. At this convention the platform of less government, less taxes, and a policy that each state should handle its own civil rights problems was supported by the Southern Western delegates.

I had a surprise when I was elected Chairman of the Permanent Organization Committee. A congressman from Ohio, Gordon Scherer, was supposed to have been chairman, the Republican National Committee had recommended him because they thought he was up for re-election.

However, it turned out that he was retiring and so he withdrew his name. I had met Tom Harris of Oklahoma City at the meeting of the Committee. He suggested that I be elected chairman and the 87 members elected me unanimously. I was already chairman of the 22 Southern members of the committee.

When I came before the National Convention, which was nationally televised to read the list of permanent officers, I was introduced as the Next Governor of Texas. I will never forget that moment in the Cow Palace since the entire Texas delegation whooped it up with the signs of Crichton for Governor of Texas.

It was obvious that the majority of delegates supported the nomination of Senator Goldwater for President. The Eastern delegation supported Nelson Rockefeller. The contest was bitter.

When the convention voted to approve the party platform, which was the platform of Goldwater, it was apparent that Goldwater would get the nomination.

Rockefeller gave a speech opposing the Goldwater platform as "Extremism." When his speech failed to generate support, the Eastern delegates proposed Governor Scranton of Pennsylvania as a moderate conservative to get the nomination.

When the roll call was made for the presidential nomination, Senator Goldwater won. Rockefeller refused to endorse the new standard bearer and his platform.

Scranton had been suggested as the Vice Presidential candidate, but Goldwater selected as his running mate Congressman William Miller, who as Republican National Chairman, had built ties to party leadership around the nation.

Peter O'Connell was greatly responsible for Goldwater's nomination, and the Texas delegates were key players. Their shouts of "Viva" and "Ole" as the convention proceeded in Goldwater's favor, were loud in the Cow Palace.

The Texas delegates retuned home tired by happy.

CHAPTER 7

AFTER THE NATIONAL CONVENTION

There was such a division between the Goldwater supporters and the Eastern Establishment that Governor Scranton of Pennsylvania hosted a meeting of the leaders of both sides, plus the governors and gubernatorial candidates at his home in Hershey, Pennsylvania in August hoping for the Republican Party to present a united front in November.

The actual meeting at Hershey, as a closed meeting attended only by Senator Goldwater, General Eisenhower, Dick Nixon, National Chairman Dean Burch, Denny Kitchel of the Goldwater campaign staff, Congressional Campaign Committee Chairman Bob Wilson, Senatorial Campaign Chairman, Thurston Morton, Governor William Stanton as host, the Republican governor, and Republican gubernatorial candidates - 38 people in all.

This was a closed meeting.

My campaign chairman, Hughes Brown, had a relationship with Governor Rockefeller of Arkansas, and as a result we were invited to fly to Little Rock, and then fly in his personal jet to the meeting. This we did, and I found the Governor very knowledgeable about the oil and gas business since he had worked as a "roughneck" in Venezuela and had other positions with the Standard Oil crowd.

After we arrived in Hershey, we went directly to the Governors mansion for drinks and dinner. The center of attention was General Eisenhower. He had such charisma that people gathered around him to hear his stories.

I remember he cautioned the gubernatorial candidates to be very careful of their language. In discussing the crime issue, he said, "At one time I made a statement that we should have some control over our "switch blades". For this remark, I alienated three ethic minorities."

I sat at a card table at which was Governor Rockefeller. I was able to establish a rapport with him by telling him about an event with John McCloy, chairman of the Chase Bank, of which Nelson's family was dominant.

I told him about a tennis match at the River Club at the match in New York, in which McCloy and I were opponents. My company at that time was negotiating a loan with Chase. My business associate Preston Peak, was a spectator at the match. McCloy served to my forehand and rushed the net. I hit the return as hard is I could, which hit McCloy in the stomach and left him breathless.

As we changed courts, Preston whispered to me, "I guess we had better start looking for another bank."

After dinner, each governor or gubernatorial candidate stood up and briefly described the issues that were important in his state.

At the end of the dinner, there was a feeling of conviviality on both sides.

Hughes and I returned, along with Governor Rockefeller in his private jet.

The Hispanic vote is most important in Texas, and in the border counties with Mexico and the Mexican newspapers are important. Accordingly, Hughes arranged a trip to Mexico City to discuss the common issues of Texas with Mexican officials in Mexico.

I was accompanied by business associates, Tom Weymouth and Ed Monteith, and we were greeted by a "Mariachi" band at the airport in Mexico City, and I was presented with a colorful sombrero.

I met with the director of tourism, and pictures were taken and the talks were published in some of the leading Mexican newspapers. I remember the headline in one paper, "Goldwater Gaining Ground", says the Texas candidate."

I now turned my attention to the state convention to be held in Austin on September 15th.

CHAPTER 8

THE REPUBLICAN STATE CONVENTION

The State Convention was on September 15, 1964, held in Austin. The delegates were eager to write a party platform that would demonstrate the differences in the Democratic Party which controlled the State and the growing Republican Party. Some 5000 delegates attended.

State Chairman, Peter O'Donnell took the lead in drafting the platform, wanting it to be synergetic with the thoughts of Senator Goldwater. The most controversy was on the Civil Rights Bill in which most of the delegates opposed bussing and thought each state should handle it's own programs. Some of my political views were adopted.

As the gubernatorial candidate, I headed the list of state candidates to speak at the convention and was labeled the "Keynote Speaker".

In my speech, I stressed the following:

(1) The need for educational reforms by increasing the salaries of the teachers, and by giving a bonus to those outstanding teachers who would become teachers in the intercity schools. (as compared to bussing), and with the state to appropriate funds for that purpose.

(2) That Texas had a water problem and a program should be initiated as to water usage in West Texas, and the need of the State to cooperate with the U.S. Corps of Engineers to build additional lakes and reservoirs.

(3) That the incumbent Governor campaigned two years ago on cutting expenses by ten percent; instead they had increased by twenty percent. As the State population increases, the State will have to provide an increase in services, but at this time that it can be accomplished by an increase in efficiency, as I, an engineer am confident that such can be done.

(4) That our basic industry is oil production and that has declined six percent in the last four years, while that in Louisiana has increased by 40 percent in the same time period. As a petroleum engineer, I would make increasing production a first priority.

(5) Parks and Wildlife. That money be appropriated for boosting tourism in the state with the establishment of more roadside stops and a better PR program. That a commission of qualified people to hear the troubles of the oyster fisherman on the gulf be established.

(6) I stressed the elimination of the power of Lyndon Johnson on state issues, and that the incumbent governor, Connally, rather than being a conservative, backed the candidate Hurbert Humphrey, who had a Socialist bent. As the campaign manager for Lyndon, he, Connally had close connections to the theft of the votes that got Lyndon elected senator. I stressed that before creating my program, I had spent several days at the Texas Research League; talked to the Texas Teachers Association, engineers with the Water Board, law enforcement officers and others. The reporters in Austin were impressed with the work done in drafting the platform, and it is interesting to note that Connally adopted some of the measures in my platform—such as "The Battered Child Syndrome" provisions.

(7) When I stressed the importance of electing Senator Goldwater, there

was a standing ovation and shouts of "Viva".

At the convention, the wife of my campaign manager, Janet Brown sold dresses with "Crichton for Governor" on them.

The principal speaker at the convention was Congressman Bill Miller, former Republican National Chairman. He was introduced by George Bush, our candidate for the U.S. Senate. Miller was a "Barry Booster."

CHAPTER 9

CAMPAIGNING AFTER THE STATE CONVENTION

Many voters do not pay attention to elections until two months before they occur. Therefore, it was important for our slate of candidates to campaign diligently during those two months before the election in November.

The Republican slate for Texas state offices, included me for Governor; Horace Houston, for Lieutenant Governor, John Trice, for Attorney General; Don Flanagan for Railroad Commissioner; Fred Newman for State Treasurer; T.E. Kennerly for Associate Justice of the Texas Supreme Count; Dallas Calmes for Controller of Public Accounts; John Matthews for Commissioner of the General Land Office, and John Armstrong, Commissioner for Agriculture.

All of these men were well qualified for the offices they were seeking.

Their reasons for seeking these offices were fueled by the desire to make Texas a two party state, and to have the state represented by a party that believed in less government and was more conservative in nature.

Peter O'Donnell, the State Chairman, decided to let the electorate see and hear these candidates, and arranged a bus trip starting in Houston and ending in the Valley, stopping at many towns en-route. Each candidate made a very short speech regarding his qualifications.

Texas is such a large state that there are different issues that are of interest in different parts of the state. In East Texas, it is oil and cattle; in West Texas, water and cotton; in the Valley, citrus and tourism; in the big cities; crime, education and taxes.

On the bus trip from Houston, I was briefed before we stopped at each town as to that town and principal political interest. Toward the end of the trip, I was so tired I fell asleep between towns, and was suddenly awakened by Horace Houston, who said, "Jack, we're here." I went to the front of the bus and stepped out to be greeted by a reporter with a microphone who said, "Welcome to our city, Mr. Crichton."

Not knowing what city I was in, I gave the very poor answer of "Thank you for the welcome, and I'm so glad to be here."

A candidate for a State office in Texas has to have incredible energy, and a good memory for names and faces.

The Republican State candidates also made a tour by plane — doing "their thing" from the tarmac of the airports.

Early in the campaign, Hughes Brown very wisely decided to use our PR funds for billboards. We received free television time when we appeared at each city.

After the state convention, all the Republican candidates for Governor west of the Mississippi river were sent to a television school in Denver, Colorado.

There we were instructed on make-ups, "wear blue shirts for TV appearances", the use of hands and body language; how to face the camera, and advice on how to avoid "freezing" when the red light on the TB camera suddenly came on. We were also put before a tough panel whose members asked us political questions, and our response was later showed to us on camera. We were given helpful advice, and to my great satisfaction the principal instructor told me, "TV is your media. Go for it".

After the State Convention, a Republican from South Texas called me and said if I were interested, he could arrange a meeting for me with former Texas Governor Coke Stevenson, who was defeated in the Senate Election of 1948 by Lyndon Johnson, whose campaign manager was John Connally. I said "yes" and he arranged for a meeting with Governor Stevenson at the Governor's ranch near Junction, Texas.

I, by myself drove to Junction, Texas from Dallas. My friend had sent me a map showing the location of the ranch. I followed the route as shown on the map, once crossing a small stream of clear water about a foot in depth, when I emerged from the trees, I saw an old fashioned ranch house with porches on each side. As I parked my car and walked up to the steps of the house, a deer ran across the lawn.

The governor was sitting in a rocking chair, and said, "welcome to our ranch. I've been expecting you. Would you like to join me in a bourbon and branch water?"

I readily agreed, and soon we were both sipping bourbon and branch water.

I said, "Governor, since my opponent in this upcoming election is John Connally, who was a big figure in getting Lyndon elected in 1948, I would be interested in hearing your side of the story."

He said, "That election seems like ages ago, but as I remember this is what happened:

"I had been declared the winner of the Senatorial race against Lyndon Johnson when suddenly votes from Box 13 in Jim Wells County controlled by George Parr, appeared and put Lyndon ahead by 87 votes. (This later caused him to be known as Landslide Lyndon.)

"I sent my campaign manager Kellis Dibrell to Jim Wells County to see about a recount of the votes. Connally had arrived before Kellis and there were no votes to be counted.

Kellis, who had been in the FBI, finally got them to let him look at the voting list. He memorized the first ten names and addresses. They were all Mexican, and Kellis later checked and six were deceased.

This was the reason for a local joke about a little Mexican boy who came crying to his mother saying, "Daddy came back from the dead to vote, but he never came by to see us."

The Governor continued: "We got an injunction from Judge Whitfield Jack in Dallas, and the case went to the Supreme Court which was in recess, and the lone member available, Justice Hugo Black held, against us.

"This election is an important part of American history for it got Lyndon in the Senate which he later controlled and was a stepping stone to his becoming President.

As for me. I was depressed for quite a while, but in retrospect it has allowed me to enjoy my ranch and my young daughter."

With that we had another bourbon and branch water, and I thanked him, and departed.

I resumed campaigning, making repeat visits to towns and cities in all parts of Texas.

I was on the podium with Senator Goldwater and George H.W. Bush a number of times. I spoke to a crowd of 30,000 when Senator Goldwater was in Houston, and to an enthusiastic crowd of five Republicans from the back of a wagon in Muleshoe, which also included a dog which had wandered by and was checking out what was going on.

One event I will never forget is when Marilyn and I were in Gladewater, Texas, for a Republican event, and a big storm hit Dallas and my mother, who was staying with our daughter in Dallas, had to be rescued by boat, along with my daughter because of the high water from White Rock Creek.

When our slate went to Amarillo, we were accompanied by Clint Walker, the TV star of "Cheyenne", whose presence related to many of the West Texas people.

The Dallas Republican Men's Club had a rally at the Baker Hotel on my birthday, October 16, where I was presented with a cake, cuff links inscribed with the GOP elephant, and a telegram from Senator Goldwater endorsing my program.

Another event I remember clearly was my returning from Corpus Christi after making a speech there. There were a number of reporters waiting for me to get off the plane. When I did, I was surrounded by them, and they wanted to know if I really meant that John Connally was the "Bag Man" for Lyndon Johnson. Unknown to me, my campaign manager, Hughes Brown had issued this press release earlier that day. The ad created quite a stir, and I told the reporters that certainly past relations between Connally and Johnson would indicate such a thing was possible.

CHAPTER 10

THE CAMPAIGN OF GEORGE H.W. BUSH FOR SENATOR

My first knowledge of George H.W. Bush was when my friend, H. Neil Mallon, a Yale icon told me about him.

During World War Two, George had entered the Navy and was trained at the Corpus Christi Naval Air Station to be a carrier pilot. On active duty in the Pacific, his plane was shot down near the Bonin Islands. He was awarded the Distinguished Flying Cross and the Air Metal on discharge from the Navy. He then attended Yale University and graduated Phi Beta Kappa in three years, and also a baseball star on the Yale Baseball team.

Having become acquainted with Texas while training in Corpus Christi, George decided to seek his fortune in Texas. With the backing of Neil Mallon, President of Dresser Industries, George moved to Midland, Texas and entered the oil business in 1948.

In partnership with the Liedke brothers, he developed a successful oil and gas drilling company.

He was active in politics in Midland, and was Republican County Chairman there.

He and the Liedke Brothers decided to go their separate ways, and the Liedke Brothers kept the oil production, and George took the drilling company. The Zapata Off Shore Oil Company. George moved to Houston in 1959, retained his interest in politics and became Harris County Republican Chairman. He came by his politics naturally since his father, Prescott Bush had been U.S. Senator from Connecticut.

In 1964, George decided to be a candidate for the U.S. Senate for the Republican Party opposing the incumbent Democratic Senator — Ralph Yarborough.

Entered in the race for the Republican nomination were Dallas attorney, Robert Morris; Dr. Milton Davis of Dallas; and Jack Cox, who had been the Republican Gubernatorial candidate two years earlier and had run a good race against John Connally, a Democrat who won and became Governor of Texas.

In the primary, George emerged on top with Jack Cox second. In the run off, George emerged the winner, and began an active campaign against Ralph Yarborough.

George was charismatic and enthusiastic and received the fervent backing of Peter O'Donnell, the State Chairman.

Having been Republican County Chairman in Midland and Houston, he had a solid base of dedicated Republican voters.

Ralph Yarborough had been feuding bitterly with Governor Connally, who had urged Congressman Joe Kilgore of the Rio Grande Valley, and former Congressman Lloyd Benson to oppose Yarborough in the Democratic primary.

George officially opened his campaign on September 17th with a statewide telecast. He carried on a consistent attack on the liberalism of

Yarborough and emphasized his own devotion to conservative principles.

George and I appeared on the podium together several times, and became friends. We discussed the conservative values of Senator Goldwater and our agreement with those views. We also discovered we both were avid tennis players.

George attracted a number of young voters, and there was a volunteer organization called "The Bush Belles"; a group of very attractive young women who did a song and dance costume in behalf of George.

I defended George with some members of right wing organizations, who accused him of being a Yankee who belonged to the Trilateral Commission and wanted a One World Government. Since I was an active member of a reserve intelligence unit, and a WWII intelligence again who accused Fidel Castro in public speeches I made a being of communist before he admitted this fact, I had some credibility. I argued that George proved himself in WWII when he risked his life as a naval aviator, and who was shot down in combat on the South Pacific. (Could anyone doubt his interest in representing the best interests of the United States in world affairs?)

The Houston Chronicle published a poll on October 1st, which indicated George had a good chance to win the election. The poll found Yarborough with a shaky lead of 51.5 percent to George's 48.0 percent. George continued to attack Yarborough for having voted for the Civil Rights Bill in the Senate, and for being politically irresponsible. The contest between the dour aging Yarborough and the young attractive Bush attracted many votes for Bush.

In the closing days of the campaign, George made appearances with Goldwater before large crowds in Houston, San Antonio, Dallas, Harlinger and Amarillo. I appeared also at those meetings.

At almost all of these functions, his attractive wife Barbara attended and was a great asset to his candidacy.

CHAPTER 11

THE CAMPAIGN OF SENATOR BARRY GOLDWATER

The campaign of Senator Goldwater started with the loss of support for the Republican nomination of Governor Nelson Rockefeller. This was triggered by the governor divorcing his wife of many years, and marrying Happy Fitler Murphy, who divorced her husband and gave up custody of her children in order to marry the Governor.

On the other hand, Senator Goldwater attracted much attention by his books, the "Conscience of a Conservative" and "Why Not Victory". Dashing, handsome, forthright and a Major General of the Air Force Reserve, he kept up his flying skills and this Arizona Senator appealed to many Americans.

Barry Goldwater was born in Arizona Territory in 1909 to wealthy parents who owned a department store in Phoenix Arizona. His father was Jewish; his mother Protestant, and Barry was reared as an Episcopalian. He enjoyed the outdoors activity in Arizona, especially fishing, hunting and rafting.

He attended Staunton Military Academy in Staunton, Virginia, and liked military life. He learned "flying" and became a pilot.

Barry left college after the death of his father to take over the operations of the family's Phoenix Goldwater store, of which he was President from 1937 to 1953. During these years he organized the Arizona Air National Guard; served on the Colorado River Commission to help bring power to central Arizona, and led a referendum for right-to-work legislation in the State.

He served in the Air Force during WWII, and at the end of the war was a Lt. Colonel.

Barry was elected to the Phoenix City Council in 1944. In 1952 he won election to the U.S. Senate.

In the Senate, he made a reputation for himself as a fervid supporter of national defense and of conservative causes.

Goldwater's conservative reputation gained the support of Peter O'Connell, the Texas Republican Chairman, and Peter became Chairman of the Draft Goldwater Committee in 1963. O'Connell was a skilled organizer, and located people around the nation who were in a position to promote the Goldwater cause with potential delegates of funds. The Committee had F. Clinton White of New York, a veteran political consultant, as its Director. Peter was successful enough to get National Republican support for Goldwater.

On the morning of November 22, 1963, a statewide poll showed that if the election were held then between Goldwater and JFK, Goldwater would carry Texas by 50,000 votes. This was important, since Texas and Illinois were the key states that got JFK elected in 1960.

The assassination of President Kennedy changed the entire political spectrum. Lyndon Johnson succeeded to the Presidency and Goldwater, if nominated, would face Lyndon in the contest for presidency.

The contest for the nomination was won by Goldwater because of solid support from the South, the Midwest and the West, and the luke warm support for Rockefeller by the Liberal Eastern Establishment.

After the nomination, Goldwater with boundless energy campaigned vigorously selling his belief in less government control, supported private enterprise, and increasing capital investment, halting the drift toward socialism and increasing our national defense.

At most rallies where Goldwater was featured there was a sign as a backdrop, "In your heart, you know he is right."

Widely quoted was his remark that "Extremism in the defense of liberty is no vice, and moderation in the pursuit of justice is not virtue."

He was hurt politically by being portrayed by a number of columnist and influential newspapers as an extremist who would provoke war with the Soviet Union. The most damaging single TV ad opposing him showed a little girl picking daises and all at once she disappears in a nuclear bomb cloud.

I joined him in Fort Worth where he spoke to several thousand people, who were from Chance Vaught, a company that had recently lost a lucrative aircraft contact to Boeing. In his forthright manner he started off his speech by saying "I sympathize with you on losing that contract, but I studied it and they offered a better deal than you folks did." I rode back to Dallas with him in his plane, and I was impressed by the feverish activity of his aides in preparing for the next appearance.

I appeared on the podium with him making speeches before him in Longview, Amarillo, Lubbock, El Paso, Fort Worth, Dallas, Houston and Corpus Christi.

CHAPTER 12

THE ELECTION

Nearly 2,700,000 votes were cast on Election Day, November 3rd. This exceeded the 2,300,000 votes cast in Texas in 1960 in the Kennedy-Nixon contest.

The Republican Party had a gathering of the candidates at the Marriott Hotel in Dallas the night of May 3rd. As election results begin to come in, the crowd lost its optimism and became quiet as it became obvious that all the Republican candidates were losing.

LBJ swamped Goldwater in Texas with 63 percent of the vote, 1,663,185 to 958,566. George Bush lost to Yarborough by a margin of 1,496,908 to 1,134,337 and I lost to Connelly 1,877,793 to 661,675.

Also losing were the two Republican Congressmen from Texas — Bruce Alger, of Dallas who had been in Congress for ten years and considered unbeatable, and Ed Foreman, a republican from West Texas who had been a star at the Republican National Convention.

Also losing were nine of the ten legislators in the Texas Legislature — only Frank Calhoun of Midland survived.

CHAPTER 13

POST MORTEM

In assaying the reasons for the total defeat of Republicans in Texas in the 1964 elections, several reasons were prominent.

The first was the guilt feeling for Texas being the place where Kennedy was assassinated. Voters tended to atone for this by backing his Vice President-Lyndon Johnson.

The second was the successful TV and media campaign against Goldwater which pictured him as being an extremist who would get the U.S. into a war against the Soviet Union, which trickled down to all the Republican candidates.

In my opinion, Goldwater would have made a great president. He would either have withdrawn our presence in Vietnam or gone whole hog to win it, instead of the piecemeal strategy of the Johnson administration that so hampered our military leaders that they in effect were not allowed to win the Vietnam conflict.

The election brought forth two politicians whose appeal in the 1964 elections would be a spring board for each to become president of the United States.

The first was Ronald Reagan. His thirty-minute speech on television on October 27, 1964 stated so succinctly the conservative principles in such an eloquent manner that he became the star of the Republican campaign. His continuance to communicate with the American public eventually landed him in the White House.

The second was George Bush. His charisma and appeal was demonstrated in the 1946 election and although losing, established his place in the Republican Party. This led him to be a congressman from Houston, Republican National Chairman, Director of the CIA, Ambassador to China, Vice President of the United States and finally President.

The election also established the foundation of the Republican Party in Texas under Peter O' Donnell's leadership and the voters were shown qualified candidates who stood for conservative principle. The influx into Texas by Republicans from other states who shared these principles finally led to the Republican Party controlling both in the House and the Senate in Texas 2003.

As for me, I had traveled some 55,000 miles to 85 cities and towns and made 275 speeches. I had also drunk hundreds of cups of coffee accompanied by the same number of cookies.

The media, including TV, radio and the newspapers were extremely fair to me. I appeared on individual television interviews in Midland, Odessa, Fort Worth, Austin, Houston Brownsville, Amarillo, Dallas, El Paso, Tyler, Abilene, Corpus Christi, Big spring and San Antonio.

I was on radio interviews from Dallas, Waco, Victoria, Dalhart, Texarkana, Bryan, McAllen, Marshall, Longview, Sherman, Midland, Odessa, Wichita Falls, Corpus Christi, Ft. Worth, Stockton, Sweetwater, Wharton, Sad Angelo, Plainview, McAllen and Amarillo.

Several newspaper political writers were especially gracious such as Allen Duckworth of the Dallas Morning News who did a half page spread on my candidacy and Carolyn Barta of the News and Eddie Barker of TV fame, from his reporting on the Kennedy assassination.

John Knaggs and Taber Ward did great work in news releases for me, and Duke Burgess did the same in PR pamphlets.

I could not have done the campaign without the support of my attractive wife, Marilyn, who accompanied me whenever possible, and my daughter Anne, and Cathy; eight and six years old. (Ann was later assistant press secretary for Governor Bill Clements.) With out the efforts of my campaign manager, Hughes Brown, and his wife Janet, I would have been lost in the political jungle. I also am indebted to all those workers who worked in my behalf.

I am also indebted to State leaders in the Republican Party such as Peter O'Donnell, Polly Sowell, Mrs. Ike Kampman (now the wife of my cousin, John Crichton), Dr. Williford, John Leedom, Jim Collins and others.

Although I lost to a popular governor with his arm in a sling from the Kennedy tragedy I think I was successful in helping to establish the Republican Party as a party that would make Texas a two party state.

I met and made friends with some wonderful people who shared my views. An example; twenty years after the election I was in an airport in Baltimore and an elderly lady came up to me and said, "I was you Precinct Chairman in Brownsville and I'll always be grateful for your effort in the 1964 election.

Such an appreciation made my efforts in 1964 worthwhile.

With every silver lining, there must be a cloud beforehand. My cloud was that as a result of my running for Governor, I lost a chance to become extremely wealthy. It happened as follows:

For a year Preston Peak, a graduate of Wharton School of Business, and I, as petroleum entrepreneurs, had been evaluating the assets of the Pure Oil Company of Palestine, Illinois.

In 1964, in the middle of my campaign, Preston informed me that the breakup value of Pure Oil Company could be $65 a share. The stock in the past had been quoted on the New York Stock Exchange as low as $30 a share. I took this information to my friend Ed Monteith, head of the Oil & Gas Department at the Republic National Bank, Dallas. He had his engineers do a study which confirmed this study. He said that the bank could possibly loan three fourths of a bid price of $65 a share.

With this information, my associate, Tom Weymouth, called his brother, George Weymouth, President of Laird and Company, Wilmington, Delaware, a company which handled some of the investments for the DuPont Group, and gave him the evaluation, and Laird and Company agreed to furnish the equity money required subject to looking at the details of the evaluation.

Mr. Robert Milligan, President of Pure Oil, had recently received a bid of $60 per share from a group headed by Carl M. Loeb, Rhodes & Company, and which included Consolidation Coal Company and Allied Chemical Company. Their bid specified after the purchase of the assets there would be new management.

George said it was imperative for me to come to Wilmington immediately. I said it was impossible for me to cancel some speaking engagements, and I would be there within a week.

A week later, Ed Monteith and I traveled to Wilmington to meet with the Laird Group. They said since there was a question regarding the depreciation, they had decided to propose a merger with the Hercules Company; a company which DuPont controlled.

The President of the Hercules Company favored the proposal, but said that he would submit it at a special board meeting, and he would require a unanimous vote by the 15 Board Members to approve the deal.

If approved, Crichton & Company would have five percent of a company worth 700 million dollars.

The special Board Meeting was called, and one director voted against it.

If I had been able to come to Wilmington immediately when called, the initial proposal would probably have been approved.

Pure Oil was later sold to Union Oil Company of California.

Thus ended the saga of the 64 election, its outcome, its cloud and its silver lining.

THE

REPORT BY THE REPUBLICAN CANDIDATE

IN THE CAMPAIGN

FOR

GOVERNOR FOR THE STATE OF TEXAS

1964

GENERAL

There were two phases in the campaign – one from the time of paying the filing fee, February 3, 1964, to the second primary, June 6, and from June 6, to the general election November 3, 1964.

During the first phase, I considered my principal job was to become known to the Republican leader and workers throughout the State. Accordingly, (I traveled almost 20,000 miles' visited some 34 different cities and towns; some of the larger ones several time) including Richardson, Houston, Waco, Victoria, Dallas, Lubbock, Midland, Oak Cliff, Corpus Christi, Austin, Pampa, Perryton, Stratford, Dumas, Amarillo, Borger, El Paso, Galveston, College Station, Fort Worth, Brownsville, McAllen, Denten, Wolfe City, Marshall, Longview, Tyler, Angleton, New Brunsfels, Bryan, Sherman, Brady, Odessa and Wichita Falls, and made 65 speeches. During this time, I also visited Governor Henry Bellmon of Oklahoma, the First Republican governor to be elected in that state, spent part of an afternoon and dinner with him in discussing various aspects of a successful campaign. I also spent hours in research on state problems, studying the state constitution, and conferring with the Republican State Legislators. For each city or town visited, I compiled a list of the state problems peculiar to that locality, plus a list of the most active Republicans in that area. My campaign office was my own business office, and my campaign manager during this first phase was Clare Weakley, Dallas.

During the second phase of the campaign, I considered that my job was to reach all the voters. Accordingly, I traveled approximately 35,000 miles to 85 separate cities and towns (several times to the larger cities), and made 210 speeches. (Included in the list of cities and towns were Dallas, Plano, Houston, Fort Worth, Victoria, Austin, Pampa, Paris, Corpus Christi, Stratton, Kingsville Midland, Andrews, Big Spring, Odessa, Kermit Pecos, Ft. Stockton, Orange, Gainesville, Corsicana, Tyler, Mason, San Antonio, Longview, Gladewater, Amarillo, Abilene, Coleman, Sweetwater, San Angelo, Kilgore, Henderson, Nacogdoches, Lufkin, Cleveland, Baytown Angleton, Rosenberg, Wharton, El Campo, Edna, Victoria, Refugio, Sinton, Alice, Mathis, Beeville, San Marcos, Denton, Lubbock, Brownfield, Levelland, Plainview, El Paso, League City, Friendswood, Alvin, Monahans, Breckenridge, Graham, Jacksboro, Decatur, McKinney, Greenville, Sulphur Springs, Mr. Vernon, Mt. Pleasant, Texarkana, Marshall, Carthage, Center, Woodville, Livingston, Bryan, College Station, Premont, Galveston, Brownsville, Harlingen, McAllen, Laredo, Del Rio, Waco, and Temple.)

Thus, in all, I traveled 55,000 miles to 85 cities and towns and made 275 speeches. For four months, I spent one half my time on the campaign, for five months all my time. I talked to crowds ranging from five adults, three children, and a stray dog which wandered in, to 30,000 people in the Colt Stadium at Houston. My wife and two children accompanied me on trips whenever possible.

In addition, the following special trips were made:

(1) San Francisco – at the Republican National Convention, I was fortunate enough to be elected to Chairman of the Permanent Organization Committee, and make the report of that committee to the convention.

(2) Mexico City – A meeting was arranged with President Elect Diaz-Ortiz in Mexico City in July. After arriving in Mexico City certain pressures resulted in cancellation of the meeting, but I did have a news conference, and explained the platform of the Republican Party to some 20 Mexican newspapers. Much publicity resulted, some favorable to Senator Goldwater. Since Mexico City papers are influential with Latin Americans in the U.S. this was though to be helpful. I also met with the head of the Mexican Tourist Bureau and discussed methods of jointly improving tourism to Mexico and Texas.

(3) Hershey, Pennsylvania – I attended the so-called Unity Conference after the National Convention, and stated what I believed the Texas Republican position to be at that conference.

(4) Denver, Colorado – I attended the Republican Gubernatorial candidates school for candidates west of the Mississippi and found it extremely helpful, especially the instruction on TV appearances.

(5) State Convention of Austin – I worked on the platform for the state convention, spent several days at the Texas Research League in

Austin, talked to the Texas State Teachers Association, engineers with the Water Board, law enforcement officers, and helped write the platform. The reporters in Austin were impressed with the amount of work done in drafting the platform, and it is interesting that Connally is pushing for some of the things we recommended – such as the "battered child syndrome" provisions.

(6) Appearances with Senator Goldwater – I met Senator Goldwater, and appeared on the podium with him, making speeches immediately before hi speech in Longview, Amarillo, Lubbock, El Paso, Fort Worth, Dallas, Houston and Corpus Christi.

(7) GOP Candidates School at Austin – this was a worthwhile school, and I was a speaker and also a student.

PUBLICITY:

The bulk of money spent in my campaign was on outdoor advertising. Since I was politically unknown it was felt that this was a must, and we had some 500 billboard signs in the state of Texas for a month before the election. Brochures and biographical pamphlets were the next largest item of expense.

I appeared on individual television appearances in Midland, Odessa, Fort Worth, Austin, Houston, Brownsville, Amarillo, Dallas, El Paso, Tyler, Abilene, Monahans, Corpus Christi, Big Spring, Laredo and San Antonio. I was on radio interviews from Dallas, Waco, Victoria, Dalhart, Texarkana, Bryan, McAllen, Marshall, Longview, Sherman, Midland, Odessa, Wichita

Falls, Corpus Christi, Ft. Stockton, Sweetwater, Wharton, San Angelo, Plainview, Center, McAllen and Amarillo.

Daily news releases were made in Austin to the Capitol Press. At each town or city I visited the newspaper, or papers on my arrival, gave me some publicity. I would like to especially commend John Knaggs, Austin for his help and advice.

FINANCE:

The total cost of my campaign was approximately $65,000, of which $35,000 came from contributions, and $30,000 from my signing notes for the amount. Most of the money came from close friends and fervid Republicans. Money raising was difficult on account of the odds against beating Connally, and the fact that most money was going to the Presidential and Senatorial campaigns.

ORGANIZATION:

My organization consisted of Hughes Brown, Campaign Manager; after phase one, Dr. Dan Sutherland, Finance manager; Paul Dearmin, Organizational Director; Taber Ward (Austin) News Releases, Publicity, and relationships in Austin; Warren Carroll speech writer and news releases; Burgess Advertising Company for Advertising; Earl Foster, Archivist; and two secretaries. The headquarters was at 7007 Preston Road, Dallas, and comprised one half a floor. A TWX machine was installed there, as was one in a small office in Austin occupied by Taber Ward. Volunteers in Dallas, consisting of some fifteen ladies helped with mailings, addresses, and other functions. Mrs. Hughes Brown was in charge of the ladies for Crichton, and designed a dress to carry out this theme. About 100 such dresses were distributed throughout the state. Robert Early, San Antonio, was in charge of Aggies for Crichton. He sent out letters to 35,000 Aggies throughout the state.

Engineers for Crichton was headed by John Jacobs, Houston, and Doctors for Crichton by Dr. Pharo, Dallas. They solicited engineers and doctors respectively.

The issues I stressed were (1) freedom of Texas for LBJ control by not reelecting his protégé, Connally. (2) Taxes would go up if Connally's programs were carried out; that he had promised a 10% cut in expenditures, and state expenses were up 20%, (3) a promise to work on cutting oil imports and beef imports and (4) firmer dealing with juvenile delinquents, emphasis on crime prevention, and harsher methods with criminals (5) work in improving Texas' share of nation's oil production (6) opposition to a state civil rights law (7) voting rights for servicemen (8) instituting a meaningful plan for state water resources (9) a program to solve traffic, problems, and cut down traffic deaths (10) opposition to the proposed all powerful state board which would absolutely control all state universities and junior colleges, but for a better coordinating board (11) for proposed teachers pay increase, emphasis on vocational training, improved graduate schools but not at the expense of undergraduate schools (12) need for a two party system in the state. Among Latin Americans I stressed that no

Latin's were on committees appointed by the Governor, and that under State Democratic programs poverty had continued among the Latin Americans. (13) Morality in government.

RESULTS:

I have not yet obtained the final results. One set of reports showed a total of 697,000 votes; another 666,000 votes. (In the election for Governor in 2000, Tony Sanchez, the losing candidate, spent 20 million dollars to get 1,8000,000 votes or $10 per vote. I spent 65,000 to get 670,000 or 10 cents per vote.

CONCLUSION:

The results of my race were determined November 22, 1963, when the President was killed and Governor Connally wounded. The attendant publicity and sympathy for both Connally and Johnson had predetermined the voting of a large segment of voters who otherwise might have voted differently. In addition, the civil rights issue caused 700,000 votes in Texas (my own estimate) out of 2,700,000 votes to vote as a "bloc." In addition, the incumbent had the advantage of getting publicity freely by dedicating a plant, or highway, and this Connally did frequently. Considering all of the factors going against us, I was not too disappointed with the final vote.

PICTURES AND CAMPAIGN LITERATURE

CRICHTON IS FOR:

1. **LOCAL GOVERNMENT** for lowest administrative cost and greatest response to community needs.

2. **MAXIMUM FREEDOM** of the individual to pursue his own affairs and to develop his creative talents.

3. **OPPOSITION TO COMMUNISM** by all means necessary to stop its spread... both internally and externally.

4. **FISCAL RESPONSIBILITY** ...or paying as we go... and spending only on predetermined priorities, such as a better educational system.

5. **TRIMMING WASTE** out of State budgets which have mushroomed under generations of one-party manipulation.

6. **A COMPETITIVE TWO-PARTY SYSTEM** which will develop the most honest and efficient government.

7. **PROTECTING TEXAS MARKETS** for livestock, agricultural, oil, and other basic products.

8. **SELLING AMERICA** on Texas attractions and actively promoting tourism to Texas.

9. **HELPING BUSINESS** prosper to create better jobs for more people.

10. **POSITIVE ACTION** to curb Texas' shocking increase in crime and delinquency.

Join Crichton's Crusade for Conservative Government!

ELECT JACK CRICHTON GOVERNOR! NOV. 3

CRICHTON

PRONOUNCED: 'CRAY-TON'

REPUBLICAN FOR GOVERNOR

Join **Crichton's Crusade** for **Conservative Government!**

JACK BELIEVES...

★ ... The leaders of our state government must be free of control by the federal bureaucracy and the White House.

★ ... Texas leaders must not remain silent when our state is smeared by demagogues either outside or inside Texas.

★ ... The basic industries of Texas — livestock, petroleum, agriculture and manufacturing — must be protected to keep Texas' economy strong.

★ ... Private investment and individual enterprise are the keys to the greatest benefits for the greatest number of people.

★ ... A favorable business climate will create prosperity for industries and better jobs at better pay for more people.

★ ... Texas' tax policy should give established Texas businesses incentives to expand, and should encourage new industries to come to Texas.

★ ... All branches of government — state, local and federal — must operate within their incomes.

★ ... Texans uphold all Constitutional provisions which guarantee equal treatment under the law for ALL citizens, but resent politically-dictated measures which will destroy the race harmony Texas has long enjoyed.

... In the critical days ahead, Texas must have a Governor who is free from federal pressures and can handle all civil conflicts firmly and fairly, as Texans want them handled.

... Communism is a menace to Texas, as it is to all the Free World. Through experience gained as an Army intelligence officer, and through first-hand study of communism in Europe, the Middle East, Africa, and Latin America, Jack Crichton has the knowledge to deal with this evil in our State.

★ ... Texas' skyrocketing crime rate calls for strong new leadership with the courage to get to the root of the moral decay which is taking a frightening toll in lives and property.

Jack was born on a cotton farm near Crichton, La., named after his grandfather. He later managed this farm as a cotton and cattle operation and understands the problems of farmers and ranchers. He owns a farm near McKinney.

Jack was in the field artillery, the Air Force and an Army intelligence officer in World War II. A major at 26, he received the Bronze Star, Air Medal and five Battle Stars. He is now a Colonel and Commanding Officer, 488th Mil. Intelligence Det., U. S. Army Reserve.

Always an honor student, Jack received his Bachelor of Science in Petroleum Engineering at Texas A&M and his Master of Science at Massachusetts Institute of Technology. He was President of the A&M Scholarship Honor Society. He is a fellow in the Texas Academy of Science and understands the problems arising in the growth of Texas as an industrial center.

Texas A&M lists Jack as one of its distinguished graduates. He is a former president of the A&M Association of Former Students and past Chairman of the A&M Development Fund.

A Personal Message to Fellow TEXANS.

SINCE the great Republic of Texas was founded more than a century ago, our state has been blessed with many responsible, energetic and constructive leaders.

Texas gained its freedom because strong-willed and determined men stood up and fought for their beliefs, their independence and their self-determination.

The generations of Texans since the Alamo have maintained that fierce independent and uncompromising spirit which has marked Texas as the state of states... big geographically, bigger in individualism and character.

But, lately there has arisen in Texas a philosophy which is strange to Texas heritage. This is the idea that says: "Don't say anything that might offend some one ... you might lose a customer or a federal center."

This attitude is understandable, but it is not traditional Texas thinking. We must stand up for Texas, rid ourselves of control from Washington and create the proper climate so that individual enterprise can be properly rewarded — thus creating better jobs for more people.

As your Governor, I pledge to take the lead in providing the proper business climate so that Texans can develop their talents and industries, and to restore in our leadership the qualities of honor, self-reliance, initiative and belief in God and country which have made Texas famous. Please join me in this great undertaking. Thank You!

Jack Crichton

Jack was an outstanding athlete in high school and at Texas A&M where he played varsity basketball, tennis and track. He is an ardent duck hunter, horseback rider and pilot.

Jack is married to the former Marilyn Berry and the father of two lovely girls — Anne, 10, and Catherine, 8. The family hobby is horseback riding on the Crichton farm near McKinney.

Jack has been deeply religious all his life. He is a former Deacon and presently an Elder in the Preston Hollow Presbyterian Church in Dallas.

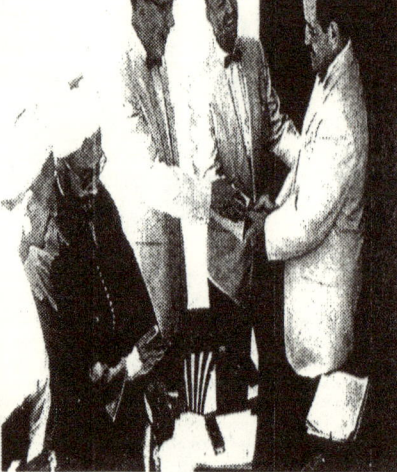

Jack began his long climb to a top spot in the oil industry by working during college as a machinist's helper and oil field worker. Since then, he has been founder, director and president of several oil firms and is currently president of Crichton & Co., and Dallas Resources, Inc.

Jack was one of four hand-picked Americans who travelled to secluded and mysterious Yemen in 1955 to secure U. S. oil rights — beating the Russians by a few days! In some parts of backwards Yemen, he was one of the first white men ever to be seen there. He is a member of the Explorers Club of New York, and has travelled extensively in Europe, South America, Africa and the Middle East.

Jack is a past National Director of the Young Presidents' Organization. He was a member of Sigma Alpha Epsilon in college, and has been active in the YMCA, Optimist International, Reserve Officers Association, Petroleum Engineers Club of Dallas (past president), a Fellow in the Texas Academy of Science, Explorers Club of New York, Texas Society of Professional Engineers and the American Institute of Mining & Metallurgical Engineers.

The Family

Mexico City

Mexico City

Alilene with Lynn Cook & Jack McGlothin

In Austin

A GREAT AMERICAN DEDICATED TO GREAT AMERICAN PRINCIPLES

The Goldwater Family together at the home of the oldest Goldwater daughter, Mrs. Joanne Ross. Left to right: (seated) grand-daughter Carolyn, Joanne Ross, Senator Goldwater, (holding grand-daughter Cynthia), Mrs. Goldwater (holding grand-daughter Alison), grandson Thomas Michael, and Peggy, Jr. (standing) Dr. Thomas Ross, Sen. Goldwater's son-in-law, Barry, Jr., Mike, and Peggy, Jr.'s husband, Richard Holt.

the unquestioned honesty of Barry Goldwater and Bill Miller and the wheeling-dealing of their opposition.

Barry Goldwater stands for:

GREATNESS OF PURPOSE — To keep the peace and extend freedom.

GREATNESS OF ACTION — To speak clearly and to be heard respectfully once again in the councils of the world.

GREATNESS OF HEART and self-restraint at home — To restore law and order, to make our streets safe, without losing liberty.

GREATNESS OF VISION — To see beyond the comforts and pleasures of the day toward the towering goals of tomorrow.

GREATNESS OF SOUL — To restore inner meaning to every man's life in a time too often rushed, too often obsessed by petty needs and material greeds, and too often controlled by the pressure of groups rather than the conscience of the individual.

Barry Goldwater seeks an America proud of its past, its ways, its dreams. His political views represent the road that America must take to preserve its ideals and halt the headlong rush to make the government master of all men.

This is the year of decision for 190 million Americans. We must decide between

BARRY GOLDWATER FOR PRESIDENT

At The State Convention

WILLIAM E. MILLER FOR VICE PRESIDENT

The Moment of Victory at the 1964 Republican National Convention

Bill Miller's lovely family comes first in his heart

Bill Miller, son of a janitor, won a scholarship and worked his way through the University of Notre Dame and Albany, N. Y., Law School during the depression. He established private law practice and served as U.S. Commissioner for Western New York State.

Bill Miller has an outstanding military record. Entering the Army in 1942 as a Private, he was later commissioned, served in Military Intelligence and was a prosecutor at the Nazi War Crimes Trials. Elected to Congress in 1950 and served continuously for 14 years. On the important House Judiciary Committee.

Bill Miller's experience in Congress and capacity for leadership was recognized when he was elected Chairman of the Republican National Committee in 1961 Miller believes: "Any government which gets so big that it can give you everything you want will also be so big that it can take everything you've got."

WILLIAM E. MILLER FOR VICE PRESIDENT

With William Miller

GEORGE BUSH FOR UNITED STATES SENATOR

George Bush is the strong candidate Texans need to defeat Ralph Yarborough in November.

With a conservative political philosophy that meshes closely with the beliefs of Barry Goldwater, George Bush will give Texas another strong, clear voice in support of fiscal integrity, states rights, a foreign policy based on unmatched military strength, and a private enterprise economy unhampered by bureaucratic meddling.

GEORGE BUSH ON THE ISSUES

Agriculture . . ."must be restored to a free market economy, subject to the basic laws of supply and demand.

Imports . . ."There should be a thorough reappraisal of our present oil and beef import programs. The ever-increasing ratio of imports is seriously damaging these two Texas industries and we must have legislation to correct the situation.

Test Ban Treaty . . ."as ratified by the Senate, will not work. I would be for a treaty with adequate, foolproof safeguards.

Federal Economy . . ."The free enterprise system must be unfettered. A strong economy means jobs, opportunity with prosperity. A controlled economy means loss of freedom and bureaucratic bungling.

Military Strength . . ."I favor a strong military posture. We cannot disarm when our enemies continually reiterate their intention to bury us."

George Bush has the qualities to make a great United States Senator for Texas — Ability, Intelligence, Integrity.

GEORGE BUSH FOR UNITED STATES SENATOR

Jack Crichton with George H.W. Bush

ABOUT THE AUTHOR

The author is an engineering graduate of Texas A&M and MIT. He is a world wide known petroleum consultant and has been a contributor to the Dallas Morning News on oil and gas happenings in Russia and the Middle East.

He is the coauthor of a book "The Dynamic Natural Gas Industry" published by the University of Oklahoma Press in 1965.

His story of "The Loss of An Aggie Ring" is on the website under J A. Crichton

He was the author of "The Political Career of Huey P Long" which won a writing contest at Texas A&M.

He has been active in Republican Party Affairs having served on the Dallas County Republican Committee and on the Republican Party State Executive Committee, and authored a number of reports to those Committees.